Sodomy
The Bad Seed

SODOMY
The Bad Seed

A journey of spiritual revelations

By
YARDLY P-J SHOULTON, MD

XULON PRESS

Xulon Press
2301 Lucien Way #415
Maitland, FL 32751
407.339.4217
www.xulonpress.com

© 2019 by Yardly P-J Shoulton, MD

All rights reserved solely by the author. The author guarantees all contents are original and do not infringe upon the legal rights of any other person or work. No part of this book may be reproduced in any form without the permission of the author. The views expressed in this book are not necessarily those of the publisher.

Unless otherwise indicated, Scripture quotations taken from the King James Version (KJV) – *public domain*.

Scripture quotations taken from the Amplified Bible (AMP). Copyright © 1954, 1958, 1962, 1964, 1965, 1987 by The Lockman Foundation. Used by permission. All rights reserved.

Printed in the United States of America.

ISBN-13: 978-1-5456-7052-1

"Knowing therefore the terror of the Lord, we persuade men." (2 Corinthians 5:11, KJV)

"For our struggle is not against flesh and blood [contending only with physical opponents], but against the rulers, against the powers, against the world forces of this [present] darkness, against the spiritual forces of wickedness in the heavenly (supernatural) places." (Ephesians 6:12, AMP)

Contents

Introduction..................................xi

1. My Journey 1
   To My Family
   My Creed
   In Remembrence

2. The Beginning Of The Story 8
   Origin Of Sodomy
   Hidden Opponent

3. Satan's Beginning 30
   The Great Coup-War In Heaven
   Satan
   Indoctrination

4. The Fall Of Man- The Trap 44

5. The Big Announcement................54
   Homosexuality
   Lesbianism
   Transgender
   Same Sex Marriage

6. Marriage.........................66

7. Virginity........................69

8. Power Of Choice 78

9. Prophesy - *To The Authority Of The Land*....... 81

10. Book Of Romans - *The Revealer* 83

11. Message To The Readers...............85

Think For Yourself *89*

A spirit has been unleashed on the earth in an aggressive, calculated, and decisive manner to take away your ability to think for yourself. The spirit of darkness in this present age is after your mind and the minds of your children. It comes through the airwaves, news, Internet, Instagram, Twitter, cell phone, television, and movies, which are spewing out their vile language, gross sexual perversion, and distortion of right living, blurring the lines of decency and obscenity with no barriers to their delivery. In any way they can, they want to get the message to you that the righteous way is not the only way. With all that is before you, you, the reader, must have the conviction and belief to say…

I can think for myself.

Introduction

My first book is being written as the Lord has instructed me. I dedicate this book to the Heflin family, founders of Calvary Pentecostal Camp (CPT), Ashland, Virginia, who were the molders, the hands that firmed my destiny in Christ. They imparted into me a life of prayer, service to others, and humility. The Heflin's taught me that a heart filled with love and compassion for humanity is fertile ground for winning souls. This set the foundation for the Holy Spirit to draw men unto Himself. They taught me to press into worship until the glory came, thereby hearing and seeing the presence of God made manifest. They stirred within my life the gifts and calling of God that were activated when I began to practice medicine. These gifts have allowed me to step into the lives of people from all over the world that I encountered during these many years of medical practice. Untold numbers of lives have come to know Jesus Christ through my life, which was changed when I experienced the love, grace, mercy, and forgiveness of my Lord and Savior, Jesus Christ. The Heflin's greatest desire was to see each believer come into the fullness of their destiny in God. It is a testimony to their ministry that believers were anointed to preach the gospel, stirring the gifts that are within each of us. We were empowered to go to the nations and our communities and to become instruments of God's power, thereby fulfilling the great commission that Jesus Christ gave to us: "Go into all the nations and make disciples of men baptizing them in the name of the Father, the son and of the Holy Spirit" (Matthew 28:18-20).

The Heflin family served God sacrificially, but they were rich in heaven's bank. Wallace Heflin Jr. gave me this command: "If the Holy Ghost is in you, do it." The next command was, "Open up." More than thirty years later, I am still "doing it," and I am still opening up the glorious realm of my God to all I encounter. My life has been one of service to the cross of Jesus Christ. I will never know my full impact on Earth, but I am sure it will be part of the crown that the Heflin's shall receive on that great day. Dr. Sarah Jane Lowder is now the director and pastor of CPT, and I say to you, Pastor Jane, "I love you and I am here for you as I was for the Heflin's." The legacy continues.

My Journey

During the last year of my internal medicine rotation, a young lady began to minister to me on the medical ward as I went through a trying time in my life. She opened the Scriptures and shared the gospel of Jesus Christ over many months. The scales were removed from my eyes, my ears opened to the gospel, and I accepted Jesus Christ as my Lord and Savior. I was born again and baptized in September 1986. The process fashioned me in the Master's hand, broke me on the potters' wheel, and molded me for His purpose to become a vessel of honor in the kingdom of God and of his Christ.

I graduated in June 1986 from a three-year internal medicine residency program and began working as a licensed physician with a medical group. That assignment lasted twenty-five years until the Lord called me into private practice in 2012. I have been practicing medicine now for thirty three years. I have had the privilege and honor of having the Holy Spirit fully operational since I began practicing medicine in July 1986. The Holy Spirit himself became my close advisor, mentor, confidant, and friend. For thirty years, He has overseen thousands of cases that I have presided over. When I began to practice medicine, I worked in the emergency room where I received revelations about the issue of sodomy that form the foundation of this book.

The information I share in this book comes from my own experiences, cases and my own personal convictions. This book does not endorse any specific ministry. I do not endorse any specific affiliations. This is my story. This is my journey.

To My Family

I dedicate this book to my family: to my children, who are the fruit of my womb and my inheritance from the Lord. You are all blessed, empowered, and equipped for warfare in your generation. To my husband, who bore the heat of the day to ensure our children would be complete in Jesus Christ as they walk their journey of life. They are all saved, sanctified, and filled with the Holy Spirit, and we commit their lives into the hands of the Lord. You all have strengthened me in my journey and taught me through the many struggles that we faced together, especially the great challenges of our special needs son, Joshua. "The fervent prayer of the righteous availeth much" (James 5:16). My eyes have seen God's hand in your lives. My Lord Jesus, I thank you for all you have done for me and all you have given me. With great persecutions and manifold rejoicings, many good gifts of blessings and miracles came through the signs and wonders that you performed in the valleys and in the mountaintop experiences of my life—you never left me. My journey continues.

This Creed I Uphold:

I believe in the Trinity, the triune God, the Father, Jesus Christ the Son, and the Holy Spirit.

I believe Jesus Christ is the Son of the living God.

I believe Jesus Christ was born of the Virgin Mary and sent by God the Father. He walked the earth, preaching the good news to the poor. He suffered a cruel mocking, a cruel death on a wooden cross for our sins. He was crucified, died, and was buried. I believe He rose again on the third day according to the Scriptures and sits at the right hand of God, making intercessions for you and me. This I believe.

I believe that Jesus Christ will come again to judge the living and the dead, and of His kingdom there will be no end. This I believe.

I believe in heaven, a place of eternal glory, a place of peace and love. It is a promised home for those who love Jesus Christ as their Savior and believe that he is the son of God. I believe there is a hell, a place of eternal torment. Hell is the place where one is separated from God forever, where light will never shine. The valley of the dead, it is the reward to all who have rejected Jesus Christ, who is the only remedy given to man for the atonement of sins. Jesus is the only hope for mankind.

> "All have sinned and come short of the glory of God" (Romans 3:23).

Scripture bears the record that Jesus Christ is the only way (John 14:6). I say again He is the only way to God the Father. Jesus himself declared, "I am the way the truth and the life. No man comes to the father but by me" (John 14:6). If anyone tries to distort this truth or compromises it to suit or appease the world's system or its culture, that person is a thief and a liar, and we know who such a person serves.

I believe the Bible is the Word of God inspired by the Holy Spirit. It was given to man to be our guide, instruction manual, blueprint, and compass to help navigate the chartered course of our lives. The Bible's contents are holy; its doctrines are sound; its words are a light to illuminate the mind, to open the heart, and to understand and acquire wisdom and knowledge by all who seek it. Judgment will fall on all those who would trifle with its sacred contents.

In Remembrance:

I dedicate this book to the memory of all my persecuted brothers and sisters throughout the world who have given their lives for the truth of the gospel. It is for the children who have shed their blood alongside their parents who refused to renounce Jesus Christ as their Lord and Savior. They were cruelly mocked, crucified, decapitated, raped, and tortured. Yet they died with joy, knowing that there was a better covenant and that they were going to a "building not made by hands." They rejoiced with an everlasting song to be counted among the chosen. To the persecuted who are still alive in prisons and suffering, I say to you in spirit, I remember you and I write this in remembrance of you.

We are fellow soldiers, conjoiners with Christ.

I remember James Wright Foley, an American journalist, whom the world watched while his captors made a mockery of him as he was decapitated. I say that his blood was not shed in vain. My prayer and hope is that the hand that held that knife to his throat and murdered him, justifying the act in the name of their god, that he may be like Saul and that God would arrest him on the road to Damascus. I pray that God would unmask him, blind him by the light of Jesus whom he persecutes, and open his eyes that he would become a forerunner of the gospel to his own people. God is righteous and will not forget the labor of love by brother Foley, and many souls shall enter the kingdom because of his sacrifice. I write this book in remembrance of him.

To the United States of America, this great land, the emblem of hope and freedom to untold millions, I dedicate this book. Lives have been changed because you embraced us. I am the daughter of immigrants who came to this country seeking a better life. They had to learn another language, and their three children had the privilege of becoming professionals in our respective fields. Our parents came here with hope, and we are the byproducts of that hope. America, you may be weary, tired; your bridal gown may be tattered, torn, and stained, but I say to you: your beauty surpasses any blemishes that you may have. You have sent thousands of missionaries from this land who have revolutionized nations for the glory of God. To you I say, I will continue to lift you up and thank God forever for you. I write this book in remembrance of you.

To the armed forces of the United States who vigilantly defend this nation, I honor you, respect you, and pray for you. You leave your families for months and years to keep the freedom of the shores of this great land. I write this book in remembrance of you.

To all the first responders who sacrifice their lives to save others, I remember you. September 11, 2001 marked my generation, as New York City was attacked by terrorists who took down the Twin Towers. Three thousand people lost their lives. I lost patients in that tragedy and continue to care for the families they left behind. We must *never forget* 9-11 and must be vigilant and watchful, for the spirit of murder is upon the land. I write in remembrance of you.

Jesus made it clear that those who are called by His name and have accepted Him as Lord and Savior have entered into a kingdom, established here on the earth, a place ruled by the monarch of heaven. This kingdom's governing body is ruled by the triune God—the Father, the Son, the Holy Spirit. This triune God is the authoritative supreme leader, the higher power who governs the tribunal of justice. Each of them has his own role of authority in this kingdom. They manifest their presence in many ways. We, as believers, are the citizens of this kingdom. We are a people called out, chosen, set apart for the Master's use. This explains why Jesus declared that as believers, we are in this world but not of this world (John 17:14-16).

This kingdom has its own monetary system; our tithes, offerings and sacrificial gifts of others are the wheels that keep this kingdom going. We bring our tithes and offerings (our first fruits) into the store house so that there will be meat in the house of God (Malachi 3:10). It is through the eyes of the Holy Spirit and the lens of my position as a citizen of this kingdom, that this book is written.

The Story Begins Here

The name of my book, *Sodomy: The Bad Seed*, was given to me by the Holy Spirit. I want to share the revelations given to me by the Holy Spirit regarding sodomy and homosexuality. Being a physician over the past thirty years, I have seen, diagnosed, and treated various challenging and difficult cases of AIDS-related diseases, and my hands have ministered to many lives. There are hundreds of cases in my mind, countless faces that I see before me that I have treated, including those who died. The conversations I've had with my patients have provided great insight into their respective worlds and their sexual practices. Those practices became evident in emergency rooms across the United States, especially in the larger cities. There are many stories I can never share, discuss, or speak about. I will make references to some cases that I took care of on the medical floors or in emergency rooms and examining rooms. The reality of those lives is the foundation of this book. I saw Satan operating through the lives of men who filled the medical wards, dying from rare opportunistic diseases destroying their immune systems.

The Story Begins Here

I began my internal medicine program as a resident before AIDS (Acquired Immune Deficiency Syndrome) had a name. I was an intern when these unusual cases began to pour into the emergency rooms and examining rooms of New York City and its surrounding hospitals; patients were coming in with rare and opportunistic infections. During my residency in my internal medicine program, New York City began to mobilize a task force to deal with bathhouses in the city (which were found to be a source of transmission of the virus that was killing people in large numbers). This virus was found to be prevalent also in the homosexual community, especially in San Francisco, where there were large numbers of HIV cases documented.

At that time, it was also documented that trans-Atlantic flights from certain states involved airline stewards who were travelling to different parts of the world and thereby appearing to spread the virus that we now know as HIV (Human Immunodeficiency Virus), or the AIDS virus. It became apparent that anal transmission by receptive anal intercourse between men and bisexual men having sex with women and men were the sources of transmission of this deadly virus. AIDS is a worldwide disease that has claimed many lives and continue to do so. Much is known now about HIV. AIDS is the end result of infection with the HIV virus. It needs to be noted that some heterosexual couples (men and women) who engage in vaginal intercourse also practice anal intercourse. Anal intercourse is also practiced in some cultures or religions where vaginal intercourse is forbidden or prohibited before marriage.

Transmission of the HIV virus also occurs via infected blood products and contaminated needles (drug abusers), and the virus can be transmitted from mother to infant through breastfeeding or at birth.

Once transmitted, the HIV virus destroys the immune system, exposing the infected individual to a host of ordinary and opportunistic infections and certain aggressive tumors. Years can go by before a person dies from the end-stage of the disease, which can range from a wasting type syndrome to a progressive disease affecting many organs. With the advent of antiviral medications, patients diagnosed with HIV are living longer, delaying the progression of AIDS-related complications.

There is medication available that now allows many with the disease to live productive lives. There is an ongoing worldwide campaign that continues to educate society on safe sex, condom use, and abstinence as alternatives. AIDS is still not curable, and research is still ongoing. More than thirty years have passed since AIDS was first diagnosed, and even though medication is available, in 2019, we are still diagnosing cases of AIDS caused by the HIV virus. An increase in other sexually transmitted diseases has also been reported. As young people become more sexually active at an earlier age, we are seeing the ravages of sexually transmitted diseases among the young and a growing resistance to medication against some of the diseases (even HIV). It is the responsibility of every parent and every church to stop hiding under the pretense that these issues are not occurring within the church. Our young people are being challenged with issues of this world, and they need godly counsel. Satan has marked them for destruction, to sift them as wheat. Jesus died to be the lifeline of hope. Without Him, we will not make it. The Holy Spirit was given to us after the ascension of Jesus Christ to lead us into all truth. He bears the testimony of Jesus Christ, who is the hope of all mankind and the remedy of the world's decay. Freedom for us was purchased through a cruel and brutal death on the cross. If we reject Christ, we reject our only hope to reach heaven's gate and to enter its courts with praise.

The preacher spoke in the book of Solomon, "vanity, vanity all is vanity for there is nothing new under the sun." Whatever is happening today has been from the beginning of time. There is nothing new under the sun.

The Origin of Sodomy

These are my personal reflections on sodomy, based on revelations and understanding given to me by the Holy Spirit. This is not an exhaustive review of this subject by any means. I only have the Scriptures to look to for clarity and understanding.

We need to review what the Bible says about the angelic realm and creation of man and its aftermath, as this subject relates to the beginning of creation. Whatever God created, Satan is going to pervert, pollute, curse, destroy, manipulate, ridicule, oppose, blaspheme, and shame, more importantly to dishonor God. Satan makes a mockery of anything that God says, creates, or puts His hand to. Satan raises up the mockers, scoffers, and jeerers to blaspheme the holy name of God and the glory of His being. Satan will distort the very Word of God to cripple it and make it of no effect, thereby nullifying the effectiveness of deliverance through the power of the blood of Jesus Christ and the purpose of reconciliation to God through the cross. He purposes to stand before man and positions himself as an alternate to God.

We know that from the dust of the earth, man was formed and in the image of God he was created. The breath of God brought forth a living man perfect in form and function. He was brought forth as a male with procreative abilities (Genesis 2:7).

We know from Scripture that the woman was formed from the man with an assigned female gender with its reproductive ability to procreate (Genesis 2:21-23).

Male and female He created them; the two are of one flesh. He gave them dominion to subdue the earth and to possess it (Genesis 1:27-28).

In Genesis 3, judgment is passed on the serpent for his trickery and on the woman and the man for yielding to temptation and eating the forbidden fruit from the tree of knowledge of good and evil and disobeying God's

The Story Begins Here

command. It is interesting that God speaks specifically to the woman about great sorrow that she would bear in conception and bringing forth children and her desire shall be to her husband and he shall rule over her (Genesis 3:16). God judges Adam for hearkening to the voice of his wife (Genesis 3:17). The original blueprint was that male and female were to be joined as husband and wife, as it states in Scripture. Through the Word of God, I can ascertain the woman was created with a womb anatomically structured to bring forth children, thus validating the role assigned to the female gender.

After Adam and Eve were banished from the Garden of Eden, Scripture states Adam "knew" his wife (Genesis 4:1). This word implies that sexual intercourse had taken place between the male and female, which set the course of the pattern for human reproduction. The breath of God in Adam's nostril brought living seed in his loins. The sexual act brought forth a male, Cain, to assure that creation would bring forth man in his likeness and this would forever continue as it is unto this day. Satan was there as Adam and Eve joined themselves together as God's word/prophecy of blessing, fruitfulness of the womb had come to pass (Genesis 1:27–28). What Satan saw must have drove him to madness! There Satan began to plant a seed of depravity to pervert the word and work of God concerning His perfect design of marriage: The woman was created to please the man; their joining of bodies was created in a manner to bring forth life. I believe the seed of sodomy was birthed in Satan's spirit from seeing the act of intercourse taking place between Adam and his wife Eve. Satan would introduce sodomy into the human genome to mimic vaginal intercourse. He intended to degrade the holiness of intercourse in marriage. Satan could not have known how God had planned to bring His Word and reproduction forth through the creation of Adam and Eve. Satan had to have seen its original blueprint in action for him to defile it. The inventor of evil things and works (Romans 1:30), Satan would now begin to wage war against the flesh in seductive, perverse, sensual warfare to bring man down to the lowest form of sexual depravity. He would exploit man and his seed until the end of the ages, being no respecter of persons.

Angels are created spirit beings and have a glory represented in the heavenly realm. Because they were created by God, they had the ability to reproduce as recorded in Scripture. The life of God in seed form was within them. It was forbidden for them to have sexual relationships with human beings. To do so had catastrophic effects.

"That the sons of God saw the daughters of men that they were fair; and they took them wives of all which they chose" (Genesis 6:2).

"There were giants in the earth in those days; and also after that, when the sons of God came in unto the daughters of men, and they bare children to them, the same became mighty men which were of old, men of renown" (Genesis 6:4).

"And the angels which kept not their first estate, but left their own habitation, he hath reserved in everlasting chains under darkness unto the judgment of the great day" (Jude 1:6).

Genesis 6 records "thus man began to multiply on the face of the earth."

"Violence and murder began to fill the earth. The wickedness of man was so great that God set in his heart to destroy the earth in every living thing in it." I can only assume that sodomy was part of man's sexual depravity at that time. God preserved the entire human race and the animal kingdom by saving the male and HIS female as it is recorded in Scripture to keep seed "offspring alive upon the face of all the earth. "And of every living thing of all flesh, two of every sort shalt thou bring into the ark, to keep them alive with thee; they shall be male and female" (Genesis 6:19).

Genesis 9 gives the account of God who saved Noah and his three sons and their wives: "the three sons of Noah: and of them was the whole earth overspread" (Genesis 9:19). It is through the sons of Noah that generations would be accounted for in history. The seed of sodomy lay within the loins of one of those men. It had to have been time to pass for children to be born to Noah's sons. For Canaan the son of Ham, the grandson of Noah shows up in Genesis 9:22. Who carried the bad seed of sodomy? Who did Satan use to continue/preserve its works?

Satan is the chief sodomite, the author of sodomy. He is the author of all that is impure untrue and false. He is the father of all lies, a murderer from the beginning and a blasphemer against holiness. He is the usurper of the Word of God. He is the polar opposite/antithesis of God. If angels themselves were endowed with the ability to procreate as given in Scripture (going after strange flesh), then Satan himself this created spirit also carried the ability to pass on his seed. I believe Satan himself sodomized a man as human beings began to multiply on the earth and introduced this defective seed of sodomy by sodomizing men themselves. He cannot be identified as chief sodomite unless he himself sodomized. He is the originator, the original inventor of sodomy. He is the epitome of wickedness and evil. He is the voice of mockers and scorners, twisting the Word of God and violating every holy precept of God.

Sodomy is the most grotesque form of aggression against the male assigned gender. Satan is filled with madness and blind rage, obsessed to the point of destruction. The sin in which he fell changed his nature so deeply, so perversely, that with our limited minds we cannot fully understand the depth of wickedness in this spirit who opposes and hates God. With great intensity, he unleashes evil against anything that reflects God. Since man reflects the image of God and is made in the likeness of God, this out-of-control behavior against man has widespread influence in the earth.

The Story Begins Here

In Genesis 3:14-15, God speaks to the serpent and passes judgment on his role in Adam's downfall: "And I will put enmity (open hostility) between you and the woman, and between your seed (offspring,) and her seed (offspring)" (Genesis 3:15, AMP).

Just as the angels were able to produce giants in the land through sexual relationships with the daughters of men (Genesis 6:2) and reproduced seed, could it then be possible that Satan himself has produced seed, his children who bear his likeness and are present among us unto this day?

Selah—think on these things!

Homosexual is defined as a person sexually attracted to people of one's own sex. Homosexuality is a romantic attraction, sexual attraction, or sexual behavior between members of the same sex or gender. The most common terms for homosexual people are gay for males and lesbians for female.

Sodomy is defined as anal or oral sexual intercourse with a member of the same or opposite sex. Sodomy is the sexual act of erectile male organ into a receptive anal canal of another man to simulate the act of vaginal intercourse.

Sodomy is sexual activity that is none procreative. Sodomy relates to two men who *by choic*e practice anal and oral sexual intercourse with each other. The sin of sodomy as it relates to a man is a grievous one. It is a weighty subject matter, with great ramifications and consequences in the spiritual realm. You cannot understand the issue, the subject of homosexuality, until you understand there is a spiritual realm.

The act of placing the seed of life (semen), the seed of procreation, into a place of refuse and dung, jeers in God's face. It marks the devaluation of man, created in God's image. It is *spiritual abortion*. The seed of man has life within it, the ability to procreate and replicate. Sodomy *aborts* the life that would have come into being. Instead, it is deposited in a canal of waste and dung, which becomes a grave for holy seed. Satan is a seed-killer, a spiritual abortionist. This is Satan's ultimate revenge.

Homosexuality speaks of denying and rejecting the female body, which is made for procreation. Through the seed of man legacies are made, and inheritances are passed on, as seen in the genealogy lines of history. Many cultures prize a male child's birth .They see it as evidence that their name, wealth, and status would continue on, and there are days of celebration after a male child has been born. The family's expectation is that at the appropriate time, this child will be able to keep their culture alive through continued procreation. It is the universal law of life. God created the womb of the woman to be a sacred place where the male seed would lie, preserving it, and assuring its development for the continuation of life. So holy, precious, and sacred are the seed of man that in the Old Testament when a young man spilled his seed (sperm) on the ground (coitus interruptus) because he did not want to impregnate a woman with his seed (semen), this displeased the Lord and God killed him (Genesis 38:9).

Sodomy is about a man. It is a satanic attack against the male race, making it effeminate and a mockery of itself. A man is created in the image of Almighty God and has been given the authority to rule, dominate, and walk in the highest authority. In his loins and in the male genitalia he carries his DNA, the original blueprint of life for reproduction and procreation. All that is happening in sodomy is the manifestation of Satan's hatred and attempt to totally sterilize the male race to homosexuality and to make a mockery of the definition of marriage by having men trade the vaginal opening of the woman for an anal canal. Thus man is brought to an even lower level than an animal. For Satan satisfies his passion through his continued onslaught against the male gender.

A transgender male is only a continuation of the emasculation of the male gender in a greater form. It is an expression of the male genital genocide/castration/mutilation, making eunuchs of men, reversing gender roles, purposefully bringing confusion to the sexes, cursing God and his handiwork in the creation of the male race made after his image. It's all about making the word of God a lie, making a mockery of all that it says, bringing doubt, unbelief, and causing men to rebel against his creator. The same rebellion that caused Satan's fall, casting him out of heaven, that spirit is alive and well and is working through the human race. His fate is known. Until the end, he will wage a great warfare in this now openly in your face subject of sodomy, homosexuality, and transgender. These unruly lives express themselves through Satan's influence.

The sin of sodomy is a spiritual act that speaks via its physical manifestation. It is the most gruesome form of a satanic attack against a man. Only a male can commit the act of sodomy. The anal canal is a thin membranous structure that is not made for the aggressive force of sexual intercourse, whereas the vaginal canal is a strong muscular organ that can withstand the enlargement to carry a ten-pound baby. The act of sodomy pays tribute to Satan, its author, by stripping humanity's kingly priesthood, taking away man's rule as it was originally given to him by God. The act makes a mockery of the original blessing of God; it defiles the body itself by feminizing it, making a man impotent and unable to do what the original blueprint was meant to do: to procreate and sustain life. Whatever looks like God is made by God, was spoken by God, and loved by God. Satan's motive is to steal, kill, and destroy it. He is a butcher who has no remorse for the pains inflicted. He is merciless, loveless, kills, and murders at will. He is an assassin, a hit man who goes around like a roaring lion seeking whom he may destroy/devour.

The beast of the fields made lower than man, looks on in amazement. The animal kingdom looks on in amazement, the trees of the field that clap their hands look on in amazement, creation groans in amazement to see man's lowly state.

Nature condemns sodomy and will rise up in the last day to condemn it. Creation will rise up against it and condemn it.

The Hidden Opponent

I write of Satan in the style that I do because I have had many dreams in which I encountered him face to face. These are three distinct dreams that I clearly remember.

Dream One

I had a dream many years ago. I was standing on a dock at nighttime. I remember seeing docked sailboats and boats. As I looked into the night sky filled with stars, I saw a large red dragon that filled the sky. Its size filled heaven. The dragon turned in the sky and I stood and watched this dragon circling in the sky, breathing out deafening sounds. In the next scene, I saw myself in a room in a building with my daughter Sarah (who was about thirteen at the time). There were several other people sitting on the floor and I remembered I asked them: "Are you ready? He's coming, are you ready?" I gave them the assurance that everything was going to be okay.

The next scene in my dream, I found myself in an eight-by-ten room with this dragon. I saw myself lying down on my right side, with my hands tucked under my chin and my eyes closed. I was at perfect peace. Around me there was hay, as in a stable. In the spirit, I saw the dragon looking at me intently as he moved his head back and forth, looking at me again and again. He kept rotating his head, staring at me, as if in wonderment of me. With angry and troubled eyes, he looked at me. This went on for quite a few minutes. Then he stopped moving, and I saw him open his mouth as though to blow out fire to consume me. Instead, what came out of his mouth was a cool breeze that blew upon my face. He looked at me with a troubled expression and moved his head back-and-forth, staring at me for a long time. He became angrier, and I saw him open his mouth, making sounds as he stared at me. Finally, he kicked his hind legs behind him through a brick wall, and I saw this dragon fly out into the midnight sky.

I knew this was a face-to-face encounter with Satan himself.

Dream Two

I experienced a demonic attack in my sleep that I was able to escape. I found myself hiding in a closet, which seemed to be in a basement, while looking through the veneer slot shutters of the closet door. I knew God delivered me and hid me from Satan's sight. In my dream, I asked God to open my eyes and show me

Satan. I saw in the spirit a living motion of air. It was a motion of his spirit that had no form, but I knew it was a person and I saw in the spirit the movement of air. I could see him looking for me as he kept looking around the room, and I saw him look behind him, sensing that I was there, but he could not see me, for God hid me from his sight. I saw him vibrating in this wave of air. No man can see air, but I saw Satan in this form. He stood there for a while, his eyes looking around. I knew I was in his sight, and he knew I was close and in the room. Finally, he resigned himself that I would not be found and literally floated through a closed door.

Dream Three

I dreamed that I was at an outdoor service preaching, standing on a makeshift platform, and I saw that there was an angry, heavy-set Caucasian man dressed in black. He stood at the base of the platform trying to stay out of view. His eyes were dark and angry. There was a large gathering of people at this outdoor meeting. I saw this man move from the side of the platform and stand in the middle of the crowd. As I preached and people were beginning to hear the truth of what I was saying, I saw the man blow out of his mouth a dark black cloud that began to cover the people. I saw the people (especially one young girl) hypnotized, as in a trance; they could no longer hear my words and renounced all that I was saying under the influence of that dark cloud that overtook them. I saw that man—Satan—in the crowd watching the effects of what he had just done, while the people were oblivious to his presence.

Satan is the ruler of this present world. This wicked spirit, this demon, is not one to play with. His presence is real, his character revealed, and his work manifested through his mayhem, destruction of and murderous intent toward all life. Only Jesus Christ and His blood shed at Calvary could have destroyed him, and He did. "And having spoiled principalities and powers, he [Jesus Christ] made a shew of them openly, triumphing over them in it" (Colossians 2:15).

Satan is the master of deception and lies who comes in many forms, sowing doubt and unbelief that dulls the mind of the believer and compromises his walk with God. Satan's cloud of darkness is blown over minds, lives, and situations, influencing leaders and nations. We need to know Satan's works, his devices, and his tricks so that we would not be caught unawares.

This book is not meant to exhaust the subject at hand. My desire is that your mind will be illuminated, and the darkness of demonic doctrines would be dispelled. My prayer is that I accomplished this as you read this book.

I witnessed many invented forms of evil, especially in the early years as I rotated through the hospital emergency room and later moonlighted many nights there. There are cases that can never be written or spoken about. Only a force of nature so strong, so evil, and so unnatural (not able to be comprehended by the human mind) can cause people to do the acts that some physicians have seen and treated. Satan's works are seen through the destruction of human life. His end is to defame, deform and for mankind to perish in his vile state. The seed of homosexuality will lead you to a life of a reprobate driving man further into darkness.

Case One

I remember a case on the sixth floor of the hospital ward while I was on call. This was a young man diagnosed with AIDS and already dying from its complications. He was in the isolation unit due to his infectious state. He also had a brain mass. In addition, his immune system was in a compromised state. I remember standing at the doorway of this patient's room ministering to him.

I asked him, "Do you know Jesus?"

He turned and looked at me from the edge of the bed where he was sitting and said, "Yeah I know him" in a sarcastic tone. His face filled with disgust and anger.

I finished speaking to him and continued my rounds. He died several days later from complications of AIDS and the brain mass that had been rapidly expanding, causing moderate swelling of his brain. I asked God as I reflected on our conversation. I said, "Where did he go?"

I had a dream that night of a cave. In that cave were bones and skulls of the dead that were laid out on various levels throughout that cave. I remember seeing several skulls on various levels of that cave. I heard the voice of the Lord say, "He is in the valley of the dead."

Hell is a real place. I have seen men leaving this earth screaming as they entered a dark valley where the dead who died without Jesus Christ went and where "the worm dieth not." These souls went to the valley of the dead, never to see light. They nourished themselves as they lived on this earth, craving fleshly pleasures and perverted lifestyles, gratifying their lustful appetites, and filled with all manner of wickedness and perversion. Such shall be the inheritance of all who live ungodly lives and who would die without repentance.

Case Two

Another case is so vividly imprinted in my mind.

I was on call one night, and a man was admitted and brought to the medical floor with profuse diarrhea over many days; he was suffering dehydration and had developed a wasting type syndrome. He was married with four children, the youngest being six months old. On taking a history of a person with such severe symptoms at presentation, there were certain questions that needed to be addressed, especially because this happened during the beginnings of the AIDS epidemic. So many male patients presented with severe complications due to their compromised immune systems, which were destroyed by various viruses, bacteria, and many opportunistic infections. The man denied any sexual contact outside his wife. He reluctantly signed for an

HIV test. He vehemently denied being bisexual until the lab results came back. I went back to speak with him and told him that he needed to tell me the truth, for the lab tests and stool culture results were saying something different. The results that came back were positive on the spectrum of an opportunistic infection and on the list of immune-related disorders, and he was HIV positive. He broke down and wept.

I had a chance to speak to his wife. She mentioned that there were always men at the house. He was always out with his male friends, and many men kept coming in and out of the house on a regular basis. She never thought anything of it, and there was no reason to believe that they were just more than his friends.

He had developed a severe fungal infection that was rotting out his tongue and his genitalia. He was dying.

One night, as I was making rounds, I knelt by his bedside and said these words to him: "There is still time. Confess your sins, accept Christ. He will forgive you. There is still time."

Out of that man's mouth I heard a voice say: "It's too late, it's too late, I got him now. I got him now."

The man was discharged from the hospital only to return several weeks later with an invasive infection. He was sitting on a stretcher in the emergency room, weak, unable to speak, wasting away due to his disease. It would be the last time that I saw him. He died soon after.

Case Three

I was on call at the hospital one weekend. There was a young man in isolation and on a respirator, unresponsive, dying of an invasive opportunistic pneumonia. His lungs were whited out from this pneumonia. As I stood outside his door, reading the chart, I looked through the glass, and in the corner of the room facing this patient was this presence, this person staring intently at this young man dying from his disease. This presence/person was the most beautiful creature I've ever seen. He was in white, with golden hair and clear eyes, but with the most wicked smile I've ever seen. He was sinister in his appearance. I followed this creature from the corner of the room, and he began to grow and enlarge. He grew taller and taller, right out of the room through the ceiling. And in the spirit, I saw that he kept growing as he reached the skies. His height was immeasurable, but I knew at that moment I had seen Satan disguised as the angel of light, as an illuminating deception. His beauty was incomparable, but he was corrupt because of his pride. Satan came and took that man. I remember going to the elevator where the dead young man's family was, trying to console his lover—who ultimately suffered the same fate.

There are many faces, cases, that can never be revealed or spoken about. I saw darkness in the lives of these men. What took place in the actual examination of many of these patients—what I saw, heard, and examined—is kept in my memory. Some details are too gruesome to speak of, incomprehensible to the natural mind. Exposing Satan's work will help the reader understand the spirit of darkness that lurks in the shadow of a man's life to bring him into bondage.

To embrace this lifestyle, you embrace death in both the natural and in the spiritual worlds. In some of these cases, they came to a place of no return. The voice of reason, persuasion, hope, and pleading ended as they took a path from which they could not return.

The Beginning

Understanding Satan's Beginning and His Position in the Angelic Hierarchy

This is a good place to lay the foundation of spirit beings. They are invisible to the human eye, but their influences for good or evil are felt throughout mankind. These are the powers in their respective roles that continue to bring prophecy to pass. "God is a spirit and they who worship Him must worship Him in spirit and in truth" (John 4:6).

To know this as truth we must understand that Satan is also a spirit. The heavenly host of angels are spirits. The operational forces behind the rise and fall of leaders (evil or otherwise), the influences behind works (wicked or otherwise), all bring their effects in the natural realm by influencing from the invisible plane. We have to understand this.

"Without understanding, without vision the people perish" (Hosea 4:6; Proverbs 29:18). Without understanding, vision, and knowledge, we will live our lives

The Beginning

fighting against people, against homosexuality and lesbianism, without understanding that it is not the person that performs the acts. We must first understand the spiritual influences behind human beings (influences from the invisible realm, the higher dimensions in the spiritual world), which manifest themselves on Earth. Ephesians 6:12 states: "for we wrestle not against flesh and blood but against principalities, against powers, against the rulers of the darkness of this world, against spiritual wickedness in high places."

I feel that for readers to understand the context of this book, they should have a clear concept of the players involved in spiritual warfare. You cannot begin to grasp the events that unfolded and where we are now, if we don't understand the stage that was set, the powers at play, the triumph and defeat of its main characters, unless we start at the beginning.

And it starts in Genesis 1:1, where there was a prior catastrophic event that eclipsed what God started in the beginning.

Whatever your beliefs, wherever you are in your walk of life, this book will give you facts and truths that should be shared and told. It is a real story with real events and real players, and the outcome of their triumphs and defeats is playing out in the earth. Kingdoms are clashing, and all that can be shaken is being shaken. We are the key players and are the prize that is sought on both sides. Each side is positioned through their influences, and the stage has been set for the battle for your eternal end: heaven or hell. You cannot understand the subject of homosexuality until you understand there is a spiritual foundation behind it. Otherwise, you will attack the life that is clouded by a deceptive force. We must go back to the beginning in the book of beginnings: Genesis.

The Great Coup: The War in Heaven

And God saw all that he had done and saw that it was good. But there was one present in all this, hearing and watching a man called Adam is being formed from the dust of the earth and God himself is breathing into this lifeless form his own breath. Satan watched man become a living soul. He heard God's decree for this man called Adam to have dominion and authority and to subdue the earth. Satan was present watching and waiting to reverse every word that God had ever decreed over Adam in the Garden of Eden.

In this utopia, Satan—Lucifer, son of the morning, a spirit of old, of renown, the dragon, the deceiver of all nations, of all mankind—was present. He had a bone to pick with God. It began long before the Garden of Eden. He is dark, unsurpassed in evil and unimaginable wickedness. But he was not like this in the beginning, so we must understand his past to comprehend and see his operation to this present day. Let's take a look.

What a beautiful creature! What beauty! What wonderment of this creature, who stood before the very

The Beginning

presence of God, created by God. He was an authoritative power and wielded great influence in God's realm of glory. Flawless in his creation, he possessed a beauty that cannot be described. The Scriptures speak of the glory of the angelic host (Psalm 103:19–21).

These glorious heavenly beings stood before God and worshiped Him day and night. And one chief angel was the worship leader of the heavenly glory. He was called the anointed cherub, created in perfect beauty, full of wisdom; he walked in perfection in the holy mountain of God. He was the ministering angel who ministered unto the Lord in worship, as he played songs never heard by man. There was the sound of glory that was emitted from him. There was an orchestra from within him that was in tune with the rhythm, the key, the sound of heavenly worship. He had it all. With great pomp and circumstance, he entered the throne room. With a great sound, he executed the workings of the instruments that were built within him as he ministered to God. He was respected by all the angels, untouchable. He had access to heaven in ways that no other angel did. He had a familiarity with heaven and its glory, and he conversed with God daily. He stood and ministered in the realm of glory of a holy God. He was one of God's prized possessions. This anointed cherub who led the heavenly choir in worship; at the sound of all the instruments, every angelic tongue began crying out proclaiming the holiness and majestic name of God and all its splendor. It brought all the hosts of heaven bowing on their knees as they worshiped the Lord. Even the angels Michael and Gabriel were on their knees and worshipped as this anointed and appointed cherub played instruments and sounds in perfect rhythm. All of heaven were in unison and Satan himself knelt, worshiping God, crying out, "Holy, Holy, Holy are you Lord." Smoke of incense from the worship filled the temple.

When Satan looked at God and watched the host of heaven on their knees, as the train of the Lord filled the temple, what were the thoughts and the intent of the heart of Satan to desire God's throne? It was a heart issue. It is only through revelation that we can try to understand, pulling from the spiritual world, the heart of this anointed cherub. A desire to be God and be like God was deeply embedded in his spirit. It filled his mind with madness until it became an obsession. He had forbidden desires and a lustful passion for position and power. He wanted the glory, honor, power, and authority for himself. He wanted to be God with a desire to exalt himself above the knowledge and the power of God.

Satan's desire and ambition to rise above the throne of God, to be like the most high God and to be worshiped as the most high God instantly brought catastrophic results, eclipsed with spiraling effects. This once chosen, anointed, appointed leader now became a castaway. Judged and condemned to spend eternity in hell, a place prepared just for him. Satan was stripped of his position. Disfigurement replaced his beauty. All

The Beginning

his privileges were gone. He was dismissed from leadership, fallen from grace, disgraced, dethroned, displaced, rejected. He was banished from heaven, never to return and no remedy was made for his reconciliation. The scepter of the king and his approval was no more extended to this chief leader of worship. His name was changed from the anointed cherub to Satan, the devil, Lucifer, son of the morning, the wicked one. He forfeited the glory of heaven for a pit of darkness.

There was an eyewitness account of what took place at that moment of his fall from grace that shook heaven. In Luke 10:18, Jesus Christ himself said, "I saw Satan falling like lightning (flash of) from heaven."

There had to be another sound that filled the heavens. It was a great cry from a fallen being. However, he was not going to leave heaven empty-handed. His influence managed to take a third of the angels with him, doomed with him to his fate. The control and power he commanded in heaven must have left the angels in awe. They knew he was an authoritative leader with great influence, and now a powerful opponent to God. There were the angels that remained loyal to God (those who did not break rank) who would fight their old colleague now on opposite sides. Their battles would be played out throughout history and climax at the end of the ages. The book of Revelation describes the final battle of these two angelic forces. Satan was disgruntled, angry, violent, destructive with murderous intentions. The covering of light (which he possessed in heaven) was now exchanged for permanent darkness. He wanted revenge. He wanted to get even, warring with God, contending against everything that depicts the character of God, blaspheming the holy name and the power of God.

In Ezekiel 28:12–19 and Isaiah 14:11–15, we have only a glimpse of what we can humanly understand this once perfect and anointed being:

> How art thou fallen from heaven, O Lucifer, son of the morning! how art thou cut down to the ground, which didst weaken the nations! For thou hast said in thine heart, I will ascend into heaven, I will exalt my throne above the stars of God: I will sit also upon the mount of the congregation, in the sides of the north: I will ascend above the heights of the clouds; I will be like the most High. Yet thou shalt be brought down to hell, to the sides of the pit. (Isaiah 14:11–15, KJV)

> You had the full measure of perfection and the finishing touch [of completeness], Full of wisdom and perfect in beauty. "You were in Eden, the garden of God; Every precious stone was your covering: The ruby, the topaz, and the diamond; The beryl, the onyx, and the jasper; The lapis lazuli, the turquoise, and the emerald; And the gold, the workmanship of your settings and your sockets, was in you. They were prepared on the day that you were created. "You were the anointed cherub who covers

and protects, And I placed you there. You were on the holy mountain of God; You walked in the midst of the stones of fire [sparkling jewels]. "You were blameless in your ways from the day you were created until unrighteousness and evil were found in you. "You were internally filled with lawlessness and violence, and you sinned. Therefore, I have cast you out as a profane and unholy thing from the mountain of God. And I have destroyed you, O covering cherub, from the midst of the stones of fire. Your heart was proud and arrogant because of your beauty; you destroyed your wisdom for the sake of your splendor. I cast you to the ground. (Ezekiel 28:12–19, AMP)

Satan

Satan is an illusionist, a master magician, an abortionist, a chameleon showing a coat of various colors to disguise itself, thus deceiving its prey when capturing it. He makes things appear to be truthful and believable that are not. He operates under a smokescreen to keep us from truly seeing the motive behind the works of deception. He is an imitator and a copycat; he presents the same plan, the same pattern causing the same effects, yet the church cannot discern him in plain view. His morally corrupt behavior, lewdness of speech, and graphic demonstration of lawlessness are being played out before our eyes, yet we discern him not. He is a tormenter; has no self-control, form of discipline, or

Sodomy

boundaries to call in question; righteousness; or right living. Satan's intent is to blind us. Though you have the eyes to see, you see not. He works under the cover of deception. What do you truly see? What do you perceive? What do you believe it to be? His work is in the realm of the flesh, sensual, enticing; he draws and appeals to your flesh, the appetite of it, the passions of it, and the love of it that draws man into perdition.

We must remember that Satan is a *spirit,* unseen by the eye. Those who succumb to his influence do so because he can plant thoughts and seeds in your mind that bring doubt and unbelief. The same subtle, cunning way that he used to tempt Eve in the garden that plunged her into rebellion and disobedience, is the same temptation that presents itself to every man until this day. He is the tempter who leads you via the senses, emotions, and feelings. Your eyes will see the forbidden realm of knowledge of evil; you will see that temptation that you yourself know is against God, His Word, or any righteous virtue. You will begin to doubt the foundation of what you know is true and right, and the boundaries set for a wholesome lifestyle begin to decay. The moral fiber of your being begins to break down. *Is it what the Word says really true? Is it really God? How do I know if all I have been taught is true? Did God mean what He said?* Doubt and subsequent unbelief lead to the demise of one's spiritual strength, bringing weakness and vulnerability to the mind, spirit, body, and soul. Now the captor has placed invisible chains on you, enslaved

The Beginning

you by your choice, snared by the words of your own mouth. You have no boundaries, no self-control—for you are now spiraling out of control, falling into an abyss, going deeper and deeper into a darkness, and at last the light of God, Jesus Christ fades. It is no longer is visible. You are now a reprobate.

Reprobate is defined as an unprincipled person, good for nothing, villain, a wretch, degenerate, depraved, worthless, shameless, immoral, wicked, bad, condemned, morally corrupt, selfish; one that is not known for their inner goodness, rejected, disapproved of, abandoned to their sins, corrupt minds, set aside, and refused. Reprobates are known by their character. They show forth the works of their father Satan, and they will do his works and his will. For there is no truth in them. They are known as his children and are cursed, entangled in a web that they can never escape. The one they serve seeks to destroy them. He destroys them physically when they give their will to his devices. It assures them a place in an eternal hell in the lake of fire.

Hell is defined as a place regarded in various religions as a spiritual realm of evil and suffering, often traditionally depicted as a place of perpetual fire beneath the earth, where the wicked are punished after death. It is the home of evil and condemned spirits, a place of torment, misery, or annihilation, the grave, the pit, a place of destruction, a place called Sheol, the world of the dead.

Hell is a real place. In many modern Christian churches, it is a subject not easily discussed, therefore beguiled souls are sent there. They were not equipped on earth with the knowledge of its eternal flames, so they are tormented, never knowing peace.

Jesus spoke of hell with warnings and instructions on your escape from it, and showed how to take the pathway to eternal life in a place called heaven. The way of eternal life (heaven or hell) is plainly revealed to all who seek to know it. There is nothing hidden. Jesus Christ is the way of escape for any man who choose to follow Him. Jesus Christ is the *only way* to the Father. Outside of Christ, we will perish.

Scripture gives us a key, a glimpse into Satan's view of where his destiny lies.

"You believe that God is one; you do well [to believe that]. The demons also believe [that], and shudder and bristle [in awe-filled terror—they have seen His wrath]!" (James 2:19, AMP)

Jesus spoke of hell on multiple occasions, making the way of escape by laying His life down to be the inheritance, the atonement for mankind's redemption, thus reconciling a lost world back to its Creator, back to God. Jesus did that for us. He is the remedy and only way of escape from this world's death grip. He came to set the captive free.

There is an organized invisible system that is played out on television and in the movies that depicts, horror, death, skeletons, deformed creatures, violence,

The Beginning

gruesome murders, ghosts, witches, warlocks, voodoo, séances, psychics and magicians to name a few. Many sit before televisions watching series on vampires, ghosts; or movies named after killers and murderers; thousands sit and laugh about these subjects. However, hell is no laughing matter. What is happening in the drawing rooms of millions of souls is that they are being desensitized to the dangers of a deceptive web where you no longer feel the sting of the name hell or fear it.

This is a real trick to make you believe all that is depicted is only "in the movies." Satan is showing you plainly the way of hell and its torments. Screams, hurling screams heard in movies, amusement parks, Halloween house of horrors. These are demons right before your eyes and you discern them not. You applaud their stage presence, but all along they are yoking you, choking you, drawing you into a darkness of sleepless nights, hallucinations, tormented thoughts, fears, phobias and paranoia, consuming more and more of your lives. These demons have entered your life by your permission and now the dead are playing out in the lives of the living who no longer lives but are the living dead unable to escape the presence of their stars, entertainment Hollywood style. The last screams are the ones you will make as hell prepares to take you home. That will not be a TV show or a movie.

As I have worked the emergency room over the years, I have heard the screams of the lost crying "my feet are burning" or "my hands are burning." They moaned and groaned, suffering, tormented with no peace in sight. For some, my face was the last they saw before their entrance into hell. The book of Revelation details these accounts.

Indoctrination

To indoctrinate is "to teach a person, or instruct someone, to accept a set of beliefs uncritically (without criticism) or to receive a lie."

It is to persuade someone to accept an idea by repeating it and showing it to be true. This form of "brainwashing" technique is a process, unfolding over time when Satan sees that your back door is open. Satan looks for a loophole in your life, something that is not surrendered to Christ; secrets, hidden lies, double life, silent addictions, and such. When any door is open, that operates in the soulish realm, Satan comes right over the border of your life and sets up shop without your *permission.* Any work which accommodates your flesh can call into your life the author of fleshly works—Satan himself, who has been lurking in the shadows, and you will have given him permission to operate in your life. Flesh is sensual, controlling, demanding, always directed by *self.* It's all about me. Self-centered, self-indulging, selfish—if that spirit is in you it is the same spirit that Satan fell for. What I call the *"I will"* syndrome is the same spirit in you that Satan had when rebelling against God. Your preoccupation with self will isolate you from the *cross* of Jesus Christ. Your mind will begin to be unreceptive to the gospel, its preaching, its call to repentance, humility, and submission to the will of God. This spirit allows the seeds of doubt and unbelief to enter and settle in your mind.

Indoctrination is a tool that Satan uses when the foundation of a life is not anchored on any sound doctrines or beliefs. The enemy begins to mold your mind, over time to believe something that normally one would not believe. He, Satan, begins to repeatedly asks the question, "Did God really say that?"

THE FALL OF MAN: THE TRAP

In Genesis 3:1, Satan himself came to Eve first and began a conversation with her concerning the command that God gave to Adam who spoke it to Eve about eating specifically from the tree of knowledge of good and evil.

> The Lord God took the man [He had made] and settled him in the Garden of Eden to cultivate and keep it. And the Lord God commanded the man, saying, "You may freely (unconditionally) eat [the fruit] from every tree of the garden; but [only] from the tree of the knowledge (recognition) of good and evil you shall not eat, otherwise on the day that you eat from it, you shall most certainly die [because of your disobedience]." (Genesis 2:15–17 AMP)

As you read this, it is clear God gave this command to Adam. The woman was created *after* the command was given. Adam later conveyed to Eve God's command, but what she told Satan was not all true.

Satan must have been around when Adam was standing in front of the forbidden tree and explaining to Eve God's command and its outcome if God's Word was disobeyed.

Satan is the master of indoctrinating your mind with repeated seeds of doubt about God's Word. He repeatedly asks: "Did God indeed say?", "Can it really be that God said?", "Did He really say that?"

It does not state in Scripture that God spoke to Eve about the tree of life and its forbidden fruit. I can only imagine that Adam, while showing Eve the glory of Eden and showing her all that had been done, must have relayed to Eve God's warning about the tree of life and the promise of imminent death for disobeying that command. Scripture does not describe God giving that command directly to Eve. Satan observed Eve in the garden. He was looking for the weak link between her and Adam, listening to their conversation, seeking to know their thoughts and where they stood in God's ordinance of loyalty, faithfulness, and obedience. He had been watching her and he must have had some knowledge of her conversation with Adam about the tree. Maybe she walked around the tree by herself, curious, wondering what Adam meant. There was a time that Eve was alone (Genesis 3:1), and Satan began the dialogue with a question. The serpent was more subtle (cunning, devious, calculating, shrewd, tricky, scheming, dishonest, deceitful, clever at achieving one's aim by indirect or deceitful methods) than any beast of the field which the Lord has made.

"Has God said you shall not eat of every tree of the garden?"

> And the woman said to the serpent, we may eat fruit from the trees of the garden, except the fruit from the tree which is in the middle of the garden. God said, "You shall not eat from it nor touch it, otherwise you will die." But the serpent said to the woman, "You certainly will not die! For God knows that on the day you eat from it your eyes will be opened [that is, you will have greater awareness], and you will be like God, knowing [the difference between] good and evil. (Genesis 3:2–5, AMP)

When Satan saw Eve was not grounded in the conviction of God's Word, Satan took it from there. God said nothing about "touching" the tree and that was all Satan needed to take her down and everybody else who doubts what God says.

This half-truth about God's words allowed Satan's affirmation to Eve that she would not die, but instead she would be like God in knowing all things. This conversation now began to focus on her feelings, needs, and self-satisfaction but not on a command about *death*, which Satan deliberately detoured her from. Although God's command was laced with a death threat, Satan downplayed it to her and began to play upon her feelings and emotions. A seed was planted in her mind deep enough (for the time being). Then she thought that the lie could be true. She found the tree (which would cost her life snared by the words of her mouth) and it was *delightful* to the eyes (charming, pleasant, pleasurable, enjoyable, amusing, entertaining, gratifying, splendid, wonderful, great, super, fabulous, terrific, heavenly, divine, captivating, ravishing, endearing, cute, delicious, ravishing, beautiful, pretty, dreamy).

This tree was desirable because it would make a person wise (exalting her desire for knowledge like God, to be like God), so Eve then became oblivious to the promise of death if she ate from it and she walked right into a trap. Now she would eat fruit from that forbidden tree because it would bring her to a place of greatness—to be like God. Now Adam, her husband, after listening to her rationale for its ingestion, also ate of it. Spiritual death instantaneously took place. Judgment and banishment soon were to follow. Immediately, the atmosphere changed, and their nakedness and shame were obvious now to their own eyes.

It is here that I believe Satan imparted his *bad seed* so man henceforth would have in it, the innate nature of evil and the propensity for rebellion and disobedience against God.

They hid from God in the garden, knowing they could no longer walk in the freedom of the garden as before. There was rebellion in the garden on which the judgment and wrath of God was about to be decreed.

Adam and Eve, the cunning snake, and all of creation stood before the God of eternity. God looked at his Son Jesus, who was also present, knowing the price that was going to have to be paid to bring Adam back to his original place of authority and right fellowship with God. Jesus was already positioned in *time* to enter in the physical plane of the earth to restore Adam and his seed back to the Father. He would defeat Satan the usurper, deceiver, and murderer who had infiltrated a cancerous cell of disobedience into God's perfect creation. Satan then controlled the human race. The seed of disobedience infiltrated the atmosphere of glory, causing a separation between God and man. The serpent was cursed, with a promise from God of his defeat in total destruction. The woman was cursed, her womb paying the price of the untold sorrow of bringing life into the world. Then Adam was cursed and the ground from which he came was cursed. In hardness of labor, the tilling of the land, and the sweat of his brow should a man eat bread until he returns to the ground from which he was taken. "Thou art dust and to dust thou shall return." (Genesis 3:19, KJV) Adam must have wept tears (which were unknown in glory up to that point). These original tears of his sorrow came when he saw his demise and that he was subject to the nature of this wicked creature, who now controlled Adam at his will. What anguish of the heart Adam must have had, crying "Abba, father!" without a response. There

The Fall Of Man: The Trap

was a sense of great love that was now lost; Adam felt annihilation, desperation, and deep regret.

God saw that if a man has made this choice to rebel against His command, he would try to take the tree of life and live forever. For this cause Adam and Eve were banished from the garden of Eden. Satan must have laughed to himself, watching Adam and Eve being led away with tears and anguish of heart, looking back at what was, what had been. Satan knew and had experienced the same anguish as Adam and Eve for the same sin, rebellion against and disobedience of the commands of God. No apologies could have turned back this clock, now ticking away their life span. But there was a remedy that God made for reconciliation of man to restore him to his original state of his relationship with Him.

All the players were now present. We know God was there, and Jesus was there, who gave an eyewitness account of Satan's fallen state from grace.

Adam had relinquished his authority and now it was in the hands and control of Satan. We know the accounts of generations of murder, death, jealousy, hatred, and such. For now, the seed of rebellion was sown in man.

In the Gospel of Matthew, Jesus meets up with Satan face to face to accomplish the promise God made when both were present in the Garden of Eden. Satan has been looking out for the deliverer that would redeem humanity. He had killed many a male child by using leaders and madmen such as Herod, trying to time the

Sodomy

Christ child's arrival. Satan knew He would be born of a woman and knowing God, Satan knew God means what He says and says what He means. There was no denying that God's promise was going to come to pass.

In Scripture, Matthew 4:1-10, especially verses 8-9, and Luke 4:1-13 (especially verses 5-7), give an account of this renowned Spirit of old and the Ancient of Days standing face to face, about to fight to the death for an eternal crown.

Here they stand in the mountain of temptation where Jesus was led by the Holy Spirit into the wilderness to be tempted by Satan. Jesus was about to dethrone this prince on His own turf and reestablish Adam's kingly rule forever. Here Jesus stood, and He had to be subjected to the elements of this world that were controlled by the spirit of the world. He was hungry and tired after fasting for forty days and forty nights.

Jesus was constrained in the flesh and had to answer this created spirit who was testing the sovereign God! He had Adam in mind by fulfilling his Father's plans in a way Satan never knew could happen—on a cross. For if Satan had known that challenging Jesus and leading him to the cross would cost him everything, he never would have crucified the Lord of glory. (1 Corinthians 2:8, KJV)

The desert was a fitting place to symbolize humanity's state after the fall of Adam. It showed the lifeless, barren state of mankind. Jesus the Christ, the redemptive answer of God, now stood ready to fulfill God's plan. These two powers once stood in the Garden of Eden.

Void of sleep and food, now entreated by Satan himself, Jesus listens to this spirit gloating, challenging Him, hurling the scriptures at Him. To the temptation of eating bread, throw himself down from the mountain (I believe this is the spirit of suicide).

Matthew 4:8:
> *The devil took him up on a very high mountain and showed him all the kingdoms of the world and the glory (the splendor, magnificent, preeminence, and excellence) of them [verse 9] and he said to him "these things all taken together, I will give you if you will prostate yourself before me and do homage and worship me."*

Jesus gave him the word and said, "Get thee behind me Satan it is written you shall do homage to and worship the Lord your God and him only shall you serve."

Matthew 4:11 states, "then the devil departed from him and behold angels came and ministered to him."

If you can understand the scenario that took place on that mountain, then you would understand the battle for man's soul. *Who* should man worship. To which of the two powers will you bow your knees? The meeting between Jesus and Satan set the foundation, secured the victory that was to be won. Jesus' entrance into the earth—to face death itself and overcome it—assured creation and all humanity of the ultimate victory. Jesus was the remedy. Only Jesus Christ has the power to destroy Satan and win. This is our only hope.

The quest, the thirst for power and authority and to have humanity bow to him is Satan's greatest desire. His heart's desire, the love of worship, was seen in his position before God as chief worshiper. He observed the adoration and praise that all the heavenly hosts, including himself, bowing on their knee to God who sat on the throne. He was determined to dethrone God from the heart, mind, the spirit, and the body of men. To deaden their conscience to the hope of the resurrected Christ.

Satan's fierce competition against God to assassinate God's character, His Word, and His plan of redemption is clearly seen in the chaos of our present world. His most aggressive weapon in his arsenal is against *man*, who is made in God's image. Satan's plan is to make the Word of God have no effect on man's mind. And we have a generation void of hope who are held captive to Satan's will. Satan will continue to contend with God through men, using *creation* (man) as a weapon against its own divine *creator* until the day Jesus comes. The sentiments of the spirits of good and evil are speaking and manifesting themselves visibly on the earth. If you refuse Jesus Christ as your liberator you have determined your own eternal fate.

Disobedience is the sin of rebellion. Satan's success in the destruction of man's life is based on man's belief that they can live their lives without God. They are not interested in learning God's teachings and following them. They now begin to live outside of the will of God, the way of God, and the Word of God. They have been indoctrinated into a self-absorbed life with no regard for the repercussions of their disobedience.

From this place the deceived walk deeper and deeper into the darkness of the lie they believe. Two men, two women, same-sex marriage, marriage equality, transgender, homosexuality, and lesbianism have found their place in our society by the process of indoctrination. Nothing matters but you; you are the only one that is important. It's all about your feelings, your emotions, and your needs. God has nothing to do with your happiness! You and you alone have an obligation and the responsibility to make you happy without rules, without boundaries and without *consequences*. That is a lie! You have believed a lie. You have been deceived and you are being deceived.

The doctrine of self-rule will ultimately lead you to the way of life of a reprobate. The Bible gives you both sides of the spectrum, and you are responsible for knowing what it says.

The Announcement

I often wondered why there must be an announcement, a declaration, a "newsworthy report" when someone has come "out of the closet" to declare to the world their sexual orientation? I often wondered why do they go through great lengths to introduce their sexual preference and the homosexual, lesbian, or transgender lifestyle they will engage in? Why do they feel a need to impress upon society their choice of sexual expression? Why?

Why do they feel they have to *cry* out "I am a lesbian!" or "I am gay (homosexual)!" or "I am transgender!"? Why do they go to great lengths to single themselves out, putting themselves on display and demonstrating what substituting nature's normal lifestyles for an abnormal one looks like? Why is their choice to "marry" someone of the same gender news? "For you are of your father the devil, And the lusts of your father you will do" (John 8:44, KJV).

They heed to his voice and follow the way of unrighteousness, a perverse way of living. Their father, the devil, has raised them up to be his voice to challenge and mock what is good and righteous in a society, stripping away a man's priestly authority, shutting up wombs and thus sterilizing themselves—a lifestyle that cannot stand. Well, Romans 1:18-32 was written of them. They fight against their own creator and perceive it not. Despite all the wealth that they possess, all the influence they may have, all the laws that they legislate, they fight against God and will not win. The declaration of their lifestyle and their sexual orientation is a means to infiltrate society's order. They must declare it to indoctrinate the minds of a civilized, orderly society—for they know that their sexual lifestyle is against nature. In the Old Testament, leprosy was a cursed disease that caused contamination and isolation from a community. Lepers were to live in a separate colony outside the camp and were dependent on others to help provide for them. There are many scriptures concerning leprosy. Leprosy is a disease that we know now is caused by *mycobacterium leprae*. Infection is spread by droplets from infected nasal mucosa, but prolonged close contact is required. The incubation period can be anywhere from three to fifteen years. The spectrum of disease is wide and destructive. There is usually involvement of the nasal mucosa, which may result in destruction of the face in palate, skin, various tissues of the body and the nerves, which may lead to loss of the extremities. There were strict ceremonial laws that governed those who were leprous. As they were approaching the public they had to cry out, "*Unclean, unclean!*" They warned others that they were leprous by their cry and their shame. The spirit of leprosy is in the land and is spreading among us. The voices of those declaring their sexual orientation are crying out, "*unclean, unclean*," yet we do not draw away. It's destroying the ability to think and heed to the voice of reason, so your nervous system is unable to react; you are numb to its destruction, and it deadens your conscience to wrong. Yet we move toward this disease by accepting it with no thought to its destructive eternal effect, though we are consciously aware it is an *unclean spirit*! As Delilah called out to Samson, "Awaken yourself For the Philistines are upon you Samson!" (Judges 16:20) In the same manner, the Holy Spirit is crying out to all you who may hear to "awaken yourselves and shake yourselves out of your slumber, for the spirit of leprosy is among us to destroy us."

In Summary

Two men who decide to engage in sexual activity between themselves, do so by choice. Their choice to leave the natural use of the woman and engage in non-procreative sexual acts, is a choice of their *own will*. They were not *born* that way; they have *chosen* to be this way, to behave this way. That way of life is their own sexual preference for their own personal satisfaction and gratification.

The Announcement

Two men cannot produce life. It is incompatible with creating life.

Two men cannot marry. No such thing exists.

Do not be deceived, God is not mocked [He will not allow Himself to be ridiculed, nor treated with contempt nor allow His precepts to be scornfully set aside]; for whatever a man sows, this and this only is what he will reap. For the one who sows to his flesh [his sinful capacity, his worldliness, his disgraceful impulses] will reap from the flesh ruin and destruction, but the one who sows to the Spirit will from the Spirit reap eternal life.

(Galatians 6:7-8 AMP)

Through the media, around dining tables, on social media it is reported that men who express their sexual desires with another man "were born that way." It puzzles me as to why it would be reported this way. It is human nature that when we want to justify actions that defy natural logic or nature's law of life, we try to pacify our conscience and avoid a sense of shame and wrongdoing. Thus, we attack and lash out at the only venue possible: we attack the irreversible pattern of life by denying the source of its handiwork.

When a child is about to be born, the set time of life has been fulfilled, nine months from its conception; there is great anticipation and planning surrounding a baby that is about to be born. The healthcare systems in modern society have technology that allows us to know the sex of the child before it is born. Many choose to wait until the day of the birth to learn the sex of the child. Is it a boy? Is it a girl?

The answer lies in the identifiable organ of this infant that will shortly appear. The doctor that is present at the delivery (or the midwives), will confirm if a male child was born because of the visible infantile penile organ. Likewise, the female with an infantile orifice of her vaginal canal. Please note this carefully: There are no identifiable marks on any child that has ever been born that marks that child as a homosexual with a propensity for anal intercourse, where sodomy is the coded choice for sexual expression.

God created man with DNA (or genetic coding), which ensures that the male sperm will carry the blueprint for replication. Only a man will always carry within his loins the power to reproduce life, which gives the assurance to creation of its continuity and which validates the creator and his perpetual and irreversible decree: "And God blessed Adam and eve and pronounced over them be fruitful, multiply and fill the earth and subdue it using all its vast resources in the service of God and man" (Genesis 1:28).

The life of man is in the seed. All living creatures and plants carry within them the seed for replication of life.

If Jesus Christ is the expressed image of the invisible God, then Adam is the expressed image of the invisible God who sealed His eternal power of procreation through the seed of Adam.

Lesbianism

Lesbianism by definition is a woman who is attracted to other women and engages in sexual behavior with that woman. It is defined as a woman whose emotional, romantic, and sexual energies are geared toward other women.

This defines the *choice* of the sexual behavior of a woman to express her sexual desires, her innate nature for sexual gratification (not with a man whose organ is created for her pleasure), but expresses her passions with another woman. Since neither one has the ability to penetrate the vaginal canal, there must be the *invention* of objects to satisfy its carnal desires. The mouth/oral cavity becomes the dominant organ for sexual arousal and stimulation between them. The vaginal canal that a woman is born with needs the natural use of the male penis (its erection and penetration) for the completeness of sexual union and fulfillment.

Their mind is seared, forbidding their body to be subjected to its natural use, but instead of playing out their gender role, one usually assumes the role of the man. The one who dominates in this reversal of roles is often more aggressive, violent, controlling, and dominates the sexual activities of the relationship. That's because they know within themselves that what they possess was made for the natural use of the man.

Two women who are sexually attracted to each other were not born that way. Rather, they have made the choice to seek out the same female gender to express their sexual passions and desires. It is an act of choice of sexual expression.

Two women together cannot be a union. *It is incompatible with life*. It does not exist along the cascade of human production.

Two women cannot "marry." It does not exist. It is incompatible with life. These sexual acts are non-procreative.

> "For their women exchanged the natural function for that which is unnatural [a function contrary to nature]" (Romans 1:24–26, AMP).

Transgender

The term transgender is defined as people who have a gender identity or gender expression that differs from that person's gender identity at birth. Their gender does not correspond to that person's biological sex.

Transgender people are sometimes called transsexual if they desire medical assistance to transition from one gender to another.

People who identify as transgender or transsexual are usually people who are born with typical male or female anatomy but feel as though they've been born into the "wrong body." For example, a person who identifies as transgender or transsexual may have typical female anatomy but "feels" like a male; likewise, a male who has a typical biologically assigned male anatomy but "feels" like a female.

What feelings can be in the mind and heart of a man or woman who can desire to change their biological gender and reverse the one assigned at their birth? How can they want to reverse their gender by submitting to the process of feminizing a male or masculinizing a female? These processes obliterate their original biological gender, making it unrecognizable. It is a sign of a life operating under a strong spirit of error.

This is the truth found in the Word of God:

> Because that, when they knew God, they glorified him not as God, neither were thankful; but became vain in their imaginations, and their foolish heart was darkened. Professing themselves to be wise, they became fools, and changed the glory of the incorruptible God into an image made like to corruptible man, and to birds, and four-footed beasts, and creeping things. (Romans 1:21–23 KJV)

I believe this scripture speaks of the spirit that changes the glory of creation; the glory of the human body of the *man* made in the image of God. Transgender changes the gender decreed at birth by marring and deforming it, by bringing confusion to the spirit, body, mind, and soul of that life.

Sodomy

Case One

I had a patient, a young twenty-year-old female who came several times for routine visits. She was of small frame, soft spoken with cropped hair. One day, she came to see me about wanting to "transition." I knew where she was going with this. I took an interview, asked her a few questions, and completed a physical exam. I gave her information about the specialist she needed to see based on her request. I heard the spirit of the Lord say to me as I stood in the exam room with this patient, "She is lost forever." She left and I did not see her again until months later, when I recognized her name but not the person sitting in front of me. Here was an overweight person who looked like male, with a mustache, with breasts enlarged due to her obesity. In truth, this was a masculinized female sitting in front of me. She was wearing pants and shirt like a male but did not have a deep masculine voice. Her voice still sounded like a girl's. She was depressed, "going through something," and wanted to talk to someone. I asked her a few questions and referred her to psychiatry. I have never seen her again.

This is confusion! She believed a lie by the author of all lies, Satan himself. This is the prize of Satan's regime, reversing the gender assigned at creation and using the hands of wickedness to change the glory of a woman into an imitation of a man.

God has given man free will and power of choice to do what he sees as "right" in his eyes, without anyone forbidding them. However, the hour will come when all men must give an account of the deeds done on this earth, whether they are good or evil. No one can escape it.

Same-Sex Marriage

Same-sex marriage does not exist.

It is a spirit of strong aggression against the very foundation of God's decree of a life-sustaining union of a man and a woman through the procreative act of sexual intercourse. That aggressive, mocking spirit brings total confusion into the spiritual realm. It is not enough that they want to validate their gender trade as a lesbian or a homosexual or transgender, but they demand that it should be sanctioned through a marriage ceremony. Thus, they make a mockery of the universal union of a man and woman for the purpose of creating life through their procreative sexual acts. Children are meant to assure continuity of life and human existence. Same-sex marriage is not compatible with life. The sexual passions of two people of the same sex result in nonprocreative acts that cannot produce life. Their "union" is fruitless and yields nothing. No life can ever come from the union of the same gender. God created the male and female genders and their procreative nature. Within their wombs and their loins are embedded life's provision of the sperm of the male and the female egg, a sustaining order compatible with life, assuring its viability and sustaining continued existence. The sexual acts of a man and a woman, which are byproducts of human sexuality, are *procreative acts* from which life is produced.

The concept behind "same-sex marriage" operates under a spirit of great deception. It is a strong spirit of error that influences people to believe such a lie. It carries a message of sterility, confusion, and rebellion against nature itself. It speaks of making God's Word impotent. It mocks what creation knows as its divine order. It makes the Word of God impotent and of no effect. They set themselves as the substitute for God's original decree, forcing themselves into a lifestyle that they see as an alternative.

"God's way is not the only way," cry Satan's children. They shake their fists in the face of a holy God. Satan's children are fierce, uncontrolled, and relentless in their motto that "God's way is not the only way."

Their rebellious hearts are void of wisdom, knowledge, or understanding. In gross sexual depravity, they are spiritual abortionists practicing the deeds of their father, Satan.

They are stiff-necked and spiritually deaf, unable to hear the truth.

They are in continual war against God, His Word, His truth, and His precepts, condemning themselves to eternal damnation—which is their fitting retribution. They are enemies of God.

Enmity is deep-rooted hatred. It's synonymous with hostility and animosity and indicates deep-seated

The Announcement

dislike or ill will. It suggests true hatred, either overt or concealed. Hostility implies strong, open enmity that shows itself in attacks or aggression. Animosity carries the sense of anger, vindictiveness and sometimes the desire to destroy what one hates. It conveys active prejudice or ill will, bad blood, bitterness.

Such is the way of man and the seed of enmity, a bad seed for one who rejects and rebels against the Word of God. The choice of master they decide to serve determines their fate. They are propelled in darkness while they live, their lives manifesting their hostility and the animosity to the truth of God. They reject knowledge of God, and their conscience is seared with a spirit to go against the path of good that God has provided through the saving blood of His Son, Jesus Christ. Their resistance to the way of life brings death and destruction in all their ways. They are deceived, deceiving, and being deceived, refusing the light of the gospel that would illuminate their dark path; the realm of darkness is reserved for them forever and forever.

Marriage

I'm getting married!
This is such a resounding declaration when it is made! It is exclaimed in all languages, in all cultures, with days, months, even years of preparation for the celebration! The union of a man and a woman is a major celebration in many countries with ancient traditions and cultures. They celebrate with prewedding activities, elaborate processions, songs, colorful garments, jewelry, and food.

This is done in anticipation that the family's name, inheritance, and traditions would continue via the birth of children who would carry on the family's livelihood, trade, business, and legacy. The family name would be continued by the bearing of children between the union of the man in the woman called the marriage. It is the *universal language* of procreation, when a man and a woman will come together to soon engage in a sanctioned acts of procreation—with great anticipation that children will be born of this union. The expected union of a man and woman in a marriage states that each has fully matured sexual characteristics and their bodies have matured in preparation for childbirth. The male's body has completed its sexual maturation, for his sexual organs must be full matured to impregnate the female.

The female, through the initiation of her menstrual cycle, heralds her sexual maturity. Sexual maturation has developed, and her womb is able to be impregnated and conception can take place. She is fully ready to carry a seed to maturity over nine months. When man and woman reach this stage, the birth of children born of the woman will begin to take place. Intercourse in many cultures is the marriage. The sexual act of the union is procreative, assuring that sexual maturity has been completed so that the union between the man and the woman will produce offspring. Marriage carries the hope of continued life and lifelong legacies. It is the hope of humanity. The married couple forms the foundation of the family, intending to continue to function in God's holy decree of procreation.

Anything outside of this is counterfeit: a robber and a thief. Satan is the inventor of evil intentions for mocking the way of truth, rebelling against the order of life and creation. Liar! He is always trying to usurp the Word of God, diverting souls from coming to the truth, lest they should see, hear, and be converted.

No such thing as marriage equality exists. These demonic spirits that have spent time planting these seeds in the minds of the simple, thus bringing doubt and unbelief to the truth and the belief in its lies. These demons laugh at man's weakness, failures, and the spirit of error that have led them astray. It is a tremendous force that is influencing our present culture to an extreme. Because men have bowed their knees to these doctrines of demons and devils, straying from the truth of the Word of God, they have closed up their ears, deaf to the voices of righteousness that are crying out, "Repent, for the kingdom of God is at hand" unto those that are perishing.

Heaven's Decree to Those Who Choose to Live Ungodly Lives

> And with all deceivableness of unrighteousness in them that perish; because they received not the love of the truth, that they might be saved. And for this cause God shall send a strong delusion, that they might believe a lie: That they all might be damned who believed not the truth, but had pleasure in unrighteousness.   (2 Thessalonians 2:10-12, KJV)

VIRGINITY

Keeping virginity until marriage is a teaching *lost* from the church, so that many young lives have been devastated and destroyed and youth have perished for lack of knowledge.

Virginity is a state in which a person has never engaged in sexual intercourse. It is a state of being naïve, innocent, or inexperienced in a particular context.

Cultural and strict religious traditions place special value and significance on this state, mostly toward unmarried females. It is associated with personal purity, honor, and worth. There are consequences, sometimes death, in strict religious cultures if a woman is not found to be a virgin at the time of marriage.

What's the big deal? It is a big deal and you need to understand why.

At completion of sexual maturation, the male and the female present themselves for future procreative sexual intercourse. At this stage, the male and female are both virgins, innocent in their understanding of what their mature bodies were created to do. the act of sexual intercourse is the vehicle by which life will come forth from their union. Intercourse is the oneness, the joining together, the coming together as one. It's all about the joining together. The "two shall be one flesh" is in the union.

What's the big deal?

Virginity, the purity of the body, the temple that has not been given to intercourse, will be a choice, a state of being, that every life that comes to sexual maturity must decide about their sexuality.

Jesus was born of a virgin. The book of Luke gives us an account of the conversation that took place between the angel sent by God to Mary, who was chosen to carry the child Jesus in her womb. (Luke 1:30-31, 3:4-35)

There was no seed given to Mary except for the overshadowing of the Holy Spirit. Within the womb of Mary, the male child, Jesus, followed the divine order of creation. He had to born of a woman. There was no human father for Jesus, for He was the seed of His Father, God. It was spirit. He was born by natural delivery through the birth canal of Mary. The genetic coding of this male child was Spirit. There was only one chromosome in Jesus, which came from His mother, for Jesus was God and man. Jesus fulfilled God's blueprint of creation and validated the pattern of the law of life. He could only receive the mother's genes, for there was no man and his conception as *He was Spirit*.

Jesus Himself, in order to fulfil the promise of salvation, had to come into the world the way of all mankind.

Virginity

The female at birth possesses a hymen, a thin membrane that surrounds or partially covers the external vaginal opening. It forms part of the vulva, or external genitalia, and is similar in structure to the vagina. It begins to develop in about the third or fourth month of pregnancy and remains intact until it is broken, mostly through sexual intercourse.

Hymen is a Greek word, meaning virginal membrane or thin skin. The presence in most cultures of an intact hymen defines the integrity of the marital bed.

The penalties were great in the Old Testament if you were married and not found to be a virgin. There were strict laws on morality that governed their lives, and in many countries those laws still govern cultures and societies to this day.

The tokens of virginity were the bloodstained sheets that the bride presumably handed to the parents after her first night of marriage. The evidence was the blood (Deuteronomy 22:13-17, 20-21, AMP).

The hymen is broken once there is penetration of the male organ into the vaginal canal, and usually there is blood after the penetration. This is the joining, the union, the marriage of a man and a woman. The loss of a woman's virginity begins with the first sexual act by intercourse and the loss of innocence. This begins a lifetime introduction to sexual lifestyle.

Sexual intercourse was meant to be a sacred act that unifies and consummates the legitimacy of the marital bed. It was always meant to occur within the confines of marriage. If you read Scripture, you will note that sexual intercourse is recognized as the marriage.

In certain cultures, there are no courthouses, justices of the peace, marriage certificates, prenuptials, or even wedding bands. When a young man comes into manhood and a young woman comes to a physical visible sexual maturation, there is an understanding that she is ready for marriage and to bear children. Many times, the families choose the mates.

The Western world's standards of how sexual intercourse is viewed are lenient, with no major repercussions for the act of losing virginity outside of marriage.

The Lord has given me many great revelations concerning this topic. It needs to be noted that for every act of sexual intercourse that takes place between a man and a woman, the spirit of the man enters the woman. The joining of bodies through the act of intercourse makes them one flesh. For the two shall become one. This is the scriptural definition of husband and wife. The woman receives not only a deposit of the man's seed in the act of intercourse, but also the spirit of the man.

As God created man and placed his spirit within man (Adam), the woman, now taken from man, receives the spirit of the man during the sexual act. In the act of intercourse, the man becomes a husband for the woman.

Laxity concerning sexual exploits is a big deal. There are grave spiritual consequences when a woman sleeps with a man. For all you young women who are contemplating sexual activity and giving away your virginity, *think again!*

You're still asking, "What's the big deal?"

Doing pelvic exams was a part of my medical practice for many years. There are several cases that I remembered when the Holy Spirit spoke to me as I interacted with patients.

Case One

I remember this woman sitting on my exam table and as I was auscultating her lungs, I had a vision and saw hundreds of men's hands imprinted on her back. I heard the voice of the Lord say, "She has had many lovers, and the way of sin she has known."

Case Two

As I prepared a young woman for her pelvic exam and was instructing her and positioning her for the insertion of the speculum, I heard the voice of the Lord say, "This is a pit to hell." I was so shocked by these words that were spoken to me in the spirit that I dropped the speculum. The words startled me. The patient said to me, "Are you okay?" I said yes. I got a clean speculum and got ready for the exam and I heard the Lord repeat those words to me again. And the scripture came to me: "For a prostitute is a deep pit, and an immoral woman is a narrow well" (Proverbs 23:27, AMP).

Your works and deeds are known to God. And God will reveal your secrets and your lifestyle and call everything into question so you can change your life and serve God. Though you live a double life, thinking no one knows of your past, think again. God is the revealer of secrets. These cases I have shared with you says this to you the reader: "There are no secrets before God. Your life is an open book and the God who searches out the heart, searches the deep things of a man's way."

It is difficult for a woman to come to Jesus Christ, be delivered, and be set free if her vessel is occupied by legions (for there are many men she has taken to bed). If she is tied to legions of husbands, there is no room for Christ!

Men are competitive beings. There is a fierce competition between these spirit beings that occupy her temple. She has received in herself the ways of her men vying for her attention and all their personalities making demands of her. All this happens because she was having sex and having "a good time." Others who know nothing of her past often are amazed by the multiple personalities that emerge from her various circumstances and stressful moments. They don't know that within her are lovers from her past living in the present, acting out, manifesting their ways through her temple (body).

These truths are hard to digest but are revealed to me by the Holy Spirit.

A lifestyle of casual sex becomes habitual, repetitively training the body to want more and to feed the needs of pleasure. For many, it is a struggle, a battle to

Virginity

satisfy the craving of the flesh. The flesh also has an appetite. It depends on the desire for self-gratification.

It is a big deal.

Only through the covenant of sanctification can a woman truly be restored to a place of purity and holiness. It is in this state that the work of the Holy Spirit is truly manifested.

Sanctification is the act or process of acquiring sanctity, of being made or becoming holy. To sanctify is to be literally set apart for a particular use, for a special purpose or work; to be made holy or sacred.

This process is the path of purging that takes place.

By definition, a purge is an abrupt or violent removal of a group of people from an organization or place. A purge is a way to get rid of something a person has wanted to get rid of, typically giving a sense of cathartic release, or to cleanse, clear, purify, wash, or absolve.

When a woman comes to the end of herself and decides to give her life to Jesus Christ, the process of purging begins. Every sexual act that has ever been performed in her body is removed, bringing her to a state of purity or virginity. Abstinence becomes her way of life. Even a prostitute who has received legions of men—all who have entered her—even she can find complete wholeness. She must renounce her lovers, forsake her ways, close the door to sexual sin, and receive Jesus Christ in her heart, who will rule and reign in her mortal body. He will beautify her temple to worship him in purity, holiness, and love, in spirit and in truth.

Sodomy

Jesus gave the woman who was caught in the very act of adultery the instruction to "go and sin no more." These words were the remedy to nullify her acts (works of the flesh). Sanctification was the remedy. The process of sanctification is completed when Jesus Christ is the Lord of her life. Worship is the maintenance of relationship with Christ who lives in you and sits on the throne of your heart. Stay on bended knees to He who has preserved you into His heavenly kingdom. It is the act of thanksgiving and freedom. The past is gone. Behold, I make all things new. You are a new creature in Christ. All women struggling with promiscuity, premarital sex, adultery and the like need to give their life and body to Jesus Christ. Only He can help them through the power of the Holy Spirit. There will be a tearing, wrenching of her mind, body, and soul. In the struggle is a fight, as the occupants leave one by one, until only Christ and him alone remains. She must bring her body under subjection and discipline.

The mind will play out the moments of sexual pleasures and the acts performed. She will go through a time of intense withdrawal as she battles through the journey of sanctification. She will wrestle with her many lovers as they try to remain alive in her spirit. As she keeps her body from sexual use, the strength of her husbands will begin to diminish. Jesus has fought this battle for her and becomes Lord when He is given permission, and the vessel will then become free.

This same process applies also for those who have battled addiction in any form or have any other form of loves other than Christ. You can be free of any idol that is in your life. Total freedom will come by permission to those who open the door to Jesus Christ and let him in.

Behold, He knocks at the door of your oppression and addiction. If you let Him in, He will set you free!

It is a big deal.

POWER OF CHOICE

"It's your choice."

Whenever I sit with a patient reviewing test results and discussing their health or an impending surgery or providing a referral to a specialist, these discussions all revolve around decisions that must be made concerning your care. No matter what the report, or plan of care I recommend for your good, the decisions are ultimately yours. As a physician, my job is to educate you and empower you with knowledge of your health, your disease. I set before you my opinion, concerns, my thoughts, and my proposed plans. I set before you the benefits versus the risks concerning choices to be made involving your care. Even if there is a bad diagnosis and an aggressive treatment plan is advised, even if it is to save your life, you have the right to say no.

I tell my patients your body is yours to do whatever you decide is right for you. I, as a physician, cannot impose my will over yours. You were given the power of choice and a free will to do whatever you decide. No man can override your decision without your permission. I can advise you, guide you, recommend options, refer you for second opinions, but the final decision is up to you. Even though I may feel that you are making a wrong decision or that you are going in a direction contrary to what I believe would benefit you in the long run, any decision about your life (medical or otherwise) rests solely in your hands. Your free will gives you independent reasoning so you have the power to go wherever you choose.

You need to have a clear understanding that this is a gift from God. The power to choose and follow your free will is a costly one, with eternal ramifications.

Every man is endowed with an innate ability to choose. It's the power of choice. It is the motivational force that sets a man's path in life. It defines borders and boundaries; it is the freedom, the key that allows others entrance into one's heart, mind, soul, and spirit. It alters destinies, defies reason, logic, truth, counsel, or wisdom. It resists the call for peace. It sets the environment, atmosphere for continued maintenance of visitations of powers at play in the earthly realm. The powers of good and evil are established forces that are playing out their influence over mankind. They are sources that a man draws from, drinks from, directs their lives from, and chooses from. The highway between the two are the choices that you have made that will set you on a course, a free course of your own will, to do whatsoever is right *in your own eyes*.

Your life is your own. God gave it to you to be its caretaker. Whatever lifestyle you choose to live, whatever you introduce to it, whatever doctrine you choose to believe, you have the power of choice, and these are the days of choosing.

This book that has been written on the behalf of Christ through the inspiration of the Holy Spirit to warn people of the choices that they make concerning their lifestyles.

Even on your way to hell, God will not cross your will. He will not impose His will against the choices that you have made. It is the power of free will that you possess. Choose *wisely*.

To the Authorities of the Land

I have a word for you from the Lord.

God has entrusted you to bring order and keep peace among men so that they follow the good of humanity. You have abused your powers by calling wrong right and right wrong, and in so doing you have multiplied iniquity in the land. You have legislated wickedness, your own hands bearing witness to your wicked deeds. Your own hands will testify against you in that day, for you have approved ordinances too wicked for men to bear.

The righteous are silenced, and you have paved the way for perverse, depraved minds to bring a generation of children into lawlessness and unbridled emotions. No one to correct them, no man can hinder them. They have let loose on the earth the spirit of depravity, base minds who refuse to heed reason. You have given them a voice to speak and to spread confusion, and they have the liberty to judge the righteous, to silence them and force them to heed to your doctrines of devils and demons. You have built the synagogue of Satan and him do you serve and worship. You blaspheme, curse, and mock that holy name—which is able to save you—and the ordinances of righteousness that rule the land. You close your ears from hearing truth, thereby searing your dead conscience to its damnable end. You have no fear of God or any retribution for the wickedness of your hands. Your end will be fitting: the midst of darkness is reserved for you forever. The right living of men is brought to bondage and chained to silence. The righteous cry out for justice to the Holy One who sits on the throne, who will answer their hearts' cry. You corrupt leaders, teachers of the damned, who hold the truth of God in ungodliness, you seek the praise (votes of men) to continue and nod to sin. Woe to you! Woe to you!

I am the Lord

THE REVEALER-ROMANS

The Word of God reveals the truth and lifts the veil of deception, showing the judgment and righteousness of God.

For [God does not overlook sin and] the wrath of God is revealed from heaven against all ungodliness and unrighteousness of men who in their wickedness suppress and stifle the truth, because that which is known about God is evident within them [in their inner consciousness], for God made it evident to them. For ever since the creation of the world His invisible attributes, His eternal power and divine nature, have been clearly seen, being understood through His workmanship [all His creation, the wonderful things that He has made], so that they [who fail to believe and trust in Him] are without excuse and without defense. For even though they knew God [as the Creator], they did not honor Him as God or give thanks [for His wondrous creation]. On the contrary, they became worthless in their thinking [godless, with pointless reasonings, and silly speculations], and their foolish heart was darkened. Claiming to be

Sodomy

wise, they became fools, and exchanged the glory and majesty and excellence of the immortal God for an image [worthless idols] in the shape of mortal man and birds and four-footed animals and reptiles. Therefore, God gave them over in the lusts of their own hearts to [sexual] impurity, so that their bodies would be dishonored among them [abandoning them to the degrading power of sin], because [by choice] they exchanged the truth of God for a lie, and worshiped and served the creature rather than the Creator, who is blessed forever! Amen.

For this reason God gave them over to degrading and vile passions; for their women exchanged the natural function for that which is unnatural And since they did not see fit to acknowledge God or consider Him worth knowing [as their Creator], God gave them over to a reprobate mind They are gossips [spreading rumors], slanderers, haters of God, insolent, arrogant, boastful, inventors [of new forms] of evil, disobedient and disrespectful to parents, without understanding, untrustworthy, unloving, unmerciful [without pity]. Although they know God's righteous decree and His judgment, that those who do such things deserve death, yet they not only do them, but they even [enthusiastically] *approve and tolerate others who practice them.*
(Romans 1:18–32, AMP)

The Last Message of the Book

> For we must all appear before the judgment seat of Christ; that everyone may receive the things done in his body, according to that he hath done, whether it be good or bad. Knowing therefore the terror of the Lord, we persuade men; but we are made manifest unto God; and I trust also are made manifest in your consciences. (2 Corinthians 5:10, KJV)

If you have been touched by this book, no matter who you are or what you have done or what lifestyle you are living, Jesus Christ can save and deliver you. The atoning power of the cross though the blood of Jesus Christ makes it possible for all of us to experience redemption, and freedom by:

1. Acknowledging we are sinners (Romans 3:23, 6:23)
2. Believing Jesus Christ is the Son of God who died for our sins and is the only way to God the Father (Acts 16:31; John 14:16)

3. Confessing your sins and asking Jesus to come into your heart (1 John 1:9, Romans 10:9)

The Word of God clearly states you must be born again. You need to have a relationship with the Lord, and through the power of the Holy Spirit, He will keep you in all your ways. You need to be baptized in the name of the Father and of the Son and of the Holy Spirit, making a public confession and a display, symbolizing that your old nature is being buried as you are immersed in water and you are coming up as a new man. Find a Bible-based church so you can begin to grow and know the Lord Jesus who loved you so much that He gave His life for you. The cross is the symbol of hope and the remedy, the antidote for sin for all humanity. If you want this new birth of salvation, if you want to be free from whatever binds, holds, or oppresses, pray this prayer with me:

> Father in the name of Jesus Christ, your Son, I come to you willingly acknowledging that I am a sinner who needs to be saved. I believe Jesus died for my sins through the shedding of his blood for me on the cross at Calvary. I confess and repent of all my sins to you right now and ask your forgiveness. Lord Jesus, I ask you now to come into my heart and into my life as my Lord and Savior from this day forward. Guide my life and help me to do your will. Holy Spirit of God, help me to walk this new path

of life that Jesus has made for me. I pray this prayer sincerely in the name of Jesus Christ. Amen.

If you have prayed this prayer, I welcome you into the family of God. I am now your sister in Christ in the kingdom of God, in which you are now a citizen. Find a church that teaches the Word of God in truth. The Bible is the instructional manual and your compass to chart your way and help navigate you through the course of this life. Read it daily; read it often. The way of Christendom will not always be an easy one, but it is a victorious one. You have the promise of Jesus that He will never leave you nor forsake you. Call out, cry out to Him in time of need. He is the one who will stick to you closer than a brother. My life has been forever changed since I accepted Jesus Christ in my life in 1986. I bow my knee to him, my Lord and Savior, who has preserved me for His heavenly kingdom. *Jesus is Lord!*

God's Blessings to all of you!

Dr. PJ

I thank my husband Byron, who was my co-editor. It took more than two years to write this book. After I completed the format, Byron was instrumental in editing my work. There were so many who inspired me and poured blessings into my life throughout the years, too many to name.

Special thank you to several pastors who encouraged me and prophesied it was my destiny to accomplish this monumental task.

To the Holy Spirit, I give all the glory, honor, praise, love, worship, and adoration for being the source of revelations given for this book. I was only the mind and hands that He needed to execute the writings that revealed the heart of God.

Lord Jesus, draw men to yourself. "And if I be lifted up from the earth, I will draw all men unto me" (John 12:32). Lord Jesus, I have lifted and glorified your name. Into your hands I commend the lives of all those who will seek you through this book. In Jesus' name I pray, Amen.

"I CAN THINK FOR MYSELF."

A spirit has been unleashed on the earth in an aggressive, calculated and decisive manner to take away your ability to think for yourself. The spirit of darkness in this present age is after your mind and the minds of your children. It comes through the airwaves, news, Internet, Instagram, Twitter, cell phones, television and movies which are spewing out their vile language, gross sexual perversion, and distortion of right living, blurring the lines of decency and obscenity so there is no barriers to their delivery. In any way they can, they want to get the message to you that the righteous way is not the only way. With all that is before you, you, the reader must have the conviction and belief to say…

I can think for myself!

www.ingramcontent.com/pod-product-compliance
Ingram Content Group UK Ltd.
Pitfield, Milton Keynes, MK11 3LW, UK
UKHW041944230426
12048UKWH00008B/126